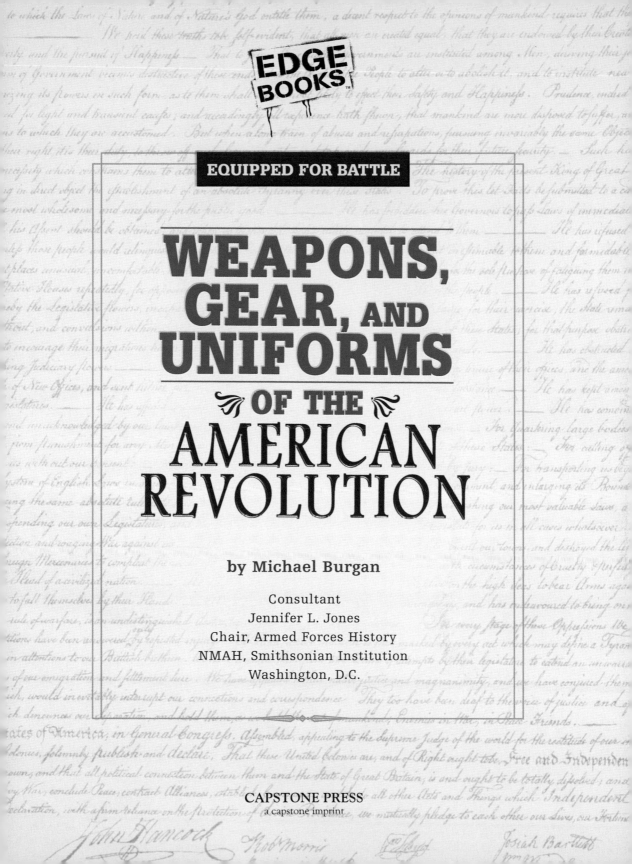

EDGE BOOKS™

WEAPONS, GEAR, AND UNIFORMS

☙ OF THE ❧

AMERICAN REVOLUTION

by Michael Burgan

Consultant
Jennifer L. Jones
Chair, Armed Forces History
NMAH, Smithsonian Institution
Washington, D.C.

CAPSTONE PRESS
a capstone imprint

Edge Books are published by Capstone Press,
1710 Roe Crest Drive, North Mankato, Minnesota 56003.
www.capstonepub.com

 Books published by Capstone Press are manufactured with paper
containing at least 10 percent post-consumer waste.

Library of Congress Cataloging-in-Publication Data
Burgan, Michael.
    Weapons, gear, and uniforms of the American Revolution / by Michael Burgan.
    p. cm.—(Edge books. Equipped for battle)
    Includes bibliographical references and index.
    Summary: "Describes the uniforms, gear, and weapons used by U.S. and British forces
during the American Revolution"—Provided by publisher.
    Audience: Grades 4–6.
    ISBN 978-1-4296-7647-2 (library binding)
    1. United States—History—Revolution, 1775–1783—Equipment and supplies—
Juvenile literature. 2. United States. Continental Army—Equipment—Juvenile literature.
3. Great Britain. Army—History—Revolution, 1775–1783—Juvenile literature. 4. Military
weapons—History—18th century—Juvenile literature. I. Title. II. Series.
E230.B87 2012
973.3'8—dc23
                                       2011028683

Editorial Credits
Aaron Sautter, editor; Ted Williams, designer; Eric Manske, production specialist

Photo Credits
Alamy: Classic Image, 9 (left), INTERFOTO, 20 (bottom); Corbis: PoodlesRock, 28;
Dreamstime: Rose-marie Henriksson, 27 (top); Getty Images: Fotosearch, 29, Superstock,
cover (battle); James P. Rowan, 23 (both), 24 (both), 25; NARA, cover (soldier); Painting by
Don Troiani/www.historicalimagebank.com, 4-5, 8, 9 (right), 10, 11 (top), 13; Shutterstock:
Dennis Donohue, 22, Jaroslaw Grudzinski, cover (pistol); The National Guard Image
Gallery Painting by Domenick D'Andrea, 15 (bottom); www.historicalimagebank.com, 11
(bottom), 12 (both), 14, 15 (top), 16, 17 (top), 18, 19 (both), 20 (top), 21 (both), 26 (both),
27 (bottom), Benninghoff Foundation, 17 (bottom)

Artistic Effects
Shutterstock: Anan Kaewkhammul, caesart, Donald Gargano, Ewa Walicka, JustASC,
maigi, Sergey Kamshylin, Susan Law Cain

Printed in the United States of America in Stevens Point, Wisconsin.
102011   006404WZS12

TABLE OF CONTENTS

THE SHOT HEARD
AROUND THE WORLD

On April 18, 1775, British troops marched out of Boston, Massachusetts, to seize the local **militia's** weapons and equipment. However, the **colonists** were prepared to defend their rights. With guns ready, the militia in Lexington waited for the Redcoats. When the two sides confronted each other, tempers flared. Without warning, shots were fired—and several colonists fell dead. The killings were just the first of the American Revolution.

militia—a group of volunteer citizens organized to fight, but who are not professional soldiers

colonist—a person who settles in a territory that is governed by his or her home country

The clash between the colonists and Great Britain had begun in 1764. The British government began raising taxes on its 13 American colonies. But no colonists sat in the British Parliament. The Americans had no say in making the tax laws that affected their lives. Many colonists became angry about taxes they felt were unfair.

In 1773 the British government passed the Tea Act. This law strengthened Britain's taxes on tea brought to the colonies. To protest the law, a group of colonists dumped thousands of pounds of tea into Boston Harbor. The Boston Tea Party angered the British, and Parliament passed new laws restricting freedoms in Massachusetts and the other colonies. Finally in 1775, the fighting in Lexington spurred the colonies to fight for independence from Britain.

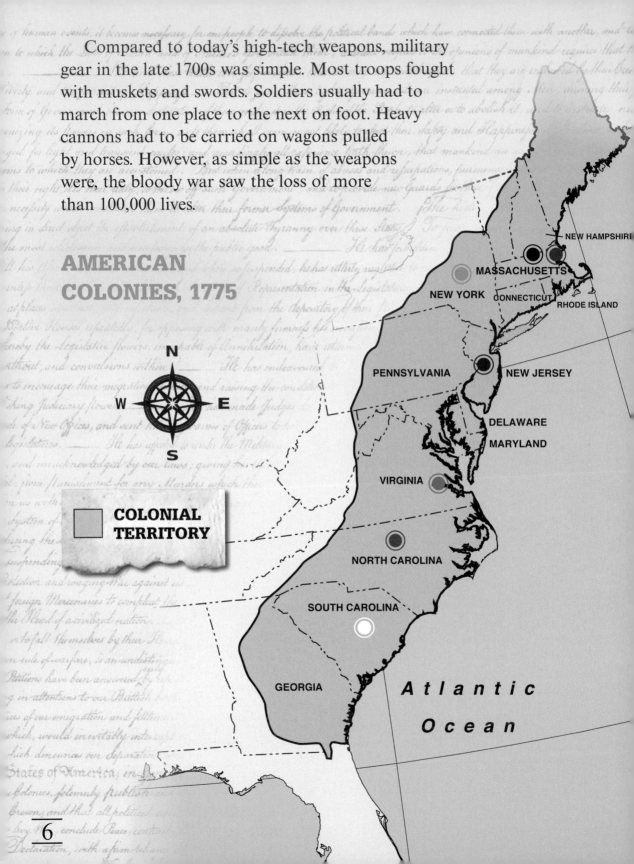

Compared to today's high-tech weapons, military gear in the late 1700s was simple. Most troops fought with muskets and swords. Soldiers usually had to march from one place to the next on foot. Heavy cannons had to be carried on wagons pulled by horses. However, as simple as the weapons were, the bloody war saw the loss of more than 100,000 lives.

AMERICAN COLONIES, 1775

N W E S

COLONIAL TERRITORY

NEW HAMPSHIRE

MASSACHUSETTS

NEW YORK CONNECTICUT

RHODE ISLAND

PENNSYLVANIA NEW JERSEY

DELAWARE

MARYLAND

VIRGINIA

NORTH CAROLINA

SOUTH CAROLINA

GEORGIA

Atlantic Ocean

MAJOR AMERICAN REVOLUTION BATTLES

● **Lexington and Concord, Massachusetts**
Fought: April 19, 1775
American casualties: 95
British casualties: 273

○ **Camden, South Carolina**
Fought: August 16, 1780
American casualties: 1,900
British casualties: 313

● **Bunker Hill, Charlestown, Massachusetts**
Fought: June 17, 1775
American casualties: 441
British casualties: 1,054

● **Guilford Courthouse, North Carolina**
Fought: March 15, 1781
American casualties: 420
British casualties: 532

● **Trenton, New Jersey**
Fought: December 26, 1776
American casualties: 441
British casualties: 1,054

● **Yorktown, Virginia**
Fought: October 6–19, 1781
American casualties: 252
British casualties: 635

● **Saratoga, New York**
Fought: October 7, 1777
American casualties: 319
British casualties: 600

BATTLE FACT

During the war, privately owned U.S. ships called privateers captured or destroyed about 600 British ships.

AMERICAN UNIFORMS

American soldiers wore a variety of clothing. Militia men and others who could not afford uniforms wore their own clothes. For those who did have uniforms, the clothing depended on a soldier's rank and specific job. Basic uniforms included a shirt, jacket, and short pants known as breeches.

CONTINENTAL SOLDIERS
The main American fighting force was the Continental Army. Early in the war, soldiers wore long, brown coats. But by 1779 most wore blue. U.S. marines wore green jackets.

HATS
Many soldiers wore a three-sided tricorn hat. Others wore cocked hats, with one part of the hat pinned up. Soldiers turned their cocked hats so the flat side faced their shooting arms. Wearing a hat this way made sure it wasn't in the way when the soldier fired his gun.

SAILORS
For daily ship life and battles at sea, sailors preferred loose, casual clothing.

FRONTIER SOLDIERS

Soldiers from the **frontier** usually wore hunting shirts. These were made of linen cloth. They were loose fitting so men could easily move their arms to fire.

CAVALRY HELMETS

American cavalry soldiers wore helmets to protect their heads if they fell from their horses. Some of the helmets had dyed horsehair attached to the top for decoration.

CONTINENTAL OFFICERS

Uniforms for officers varied. Officers' hats often included a decoration called a cockade. This small knot of colored ribbons helped show an officer's rank. Shoulder markings called epaulettes also showed an officer's rank.

frontier—the far edge of a settled area, where few people live

BRITISH UNIFORMS

British soldiers were professionals. They were expected to wear their uniforms a certain way and look their best. But their colorful, fancy uniforms weren't always practical on the battlefield. Stiff shirt collars made it hard for soldiers to turn their heads, for example. Still, certain items of clothing were useful, such as helmets and straps for holding gear.

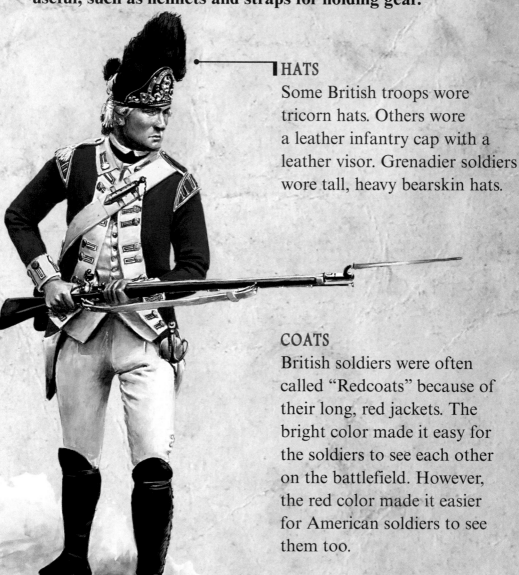

HATS
Some British troops wore tricorn hats. Others wore a leather infantry cap with a leather visor. Grenadier soldiers wore tall, heavy bearskin hats.

COATS
British soldiers were often called "Redcoats" because of their long, red jackets. The bright color made it easy for the soldiers to see each other on the battlefield. However, the red color made it easier for American soldiers to see them too.

BRITISH CAVALRY

The arrival of British cavalry marked the first time these mounted troops were used in North America. British riders often wore metal helmets.

BATTLE FACT

One group of British cavalry wore brass helmets. A white skull was painted on the front, which stood for death. The words "or glory" were underneath it.

OFFICERS' GORGETS

An officer's formal uniform included a gorget. These small decorations were originally large metal breastplates that soldiers wore for protection in battle. But by the American Revolution, officers mainly wore them as symbols of their rank. They no longer offered much protection in battle. Some American officers, such as George Washington, also wore gorgets.

GEAR FOR DAILY LIFE

Both British and American troops carried most of the gear they needed. British soldiers received supplies from the government. But American troops often had trouble getting the supplies they needed. Continental soldiers often had to make their own gear. They also captured necessary supplies from the British.

HAVERSACKS

A cloth bag called a haversack held food and items a soldier needed to eat. Larger bags were called knapsacks and had two straps, one for each shoulder.

CANTEENS

Many soldiers carried their water in wooden canteens. A few canteens were made of metal. Larger wooden kegs were sometimes carried as well.

TINDERBOX

Starting a fire outdoors was important for cooking food and keeping warm. Soldiers kept fire-starting tools in a tinderbox. It contained a flint and steel that were struck together to create a spark. The box also held small strips of cloth that caught the spark and began to burn.

BEDROLLS

Bedrolls were worn over the shoulder. The simple bedding consisted of a ground cloth and a blanket. Soldiers slept with the ground cloth under them and covered themselves with the blanket.

KNIVES

Many soldiers carried a knife for eating, a pocketknife, and a fascine knife. Fascine knives had hooked blades that were useful for cutting small tree branches.

BATTLE FACT

Fascine refers to bundles of wood tied together. Soldiers placed these bundles of wood around cannons to provide some protection for the gunners.

TOOLS FOR WAR

Marching and fighting in the war was tiring. In addition to their weapons, soldiers had to carry several tools on the battlefield. Many tools were needed to prepare and fire the soldiers' muskets. Officers had tools to keep watch over a battle. Special equipment was also used to inspire soldiers to keep fighting as the battle raged on.

CARTRIDGES

Cartridges consisted of paper wrapped around metal balls, called shot, and gunpowder. A soldier usually bit open the top of the cartridge and poured some gunpowder into the musket's pan near the trigger. The rest of the gunpowder and the shot was then poured down the gun barrel. The soldier rammed down the shot and powder with a metal rod before firing the weapon.

POWDER HORNS

Some soldiers kept their shot and gunpowder separate. The powder was stored in hollow horns taken from a cow or other animal. The horns often had designs, pictures, or even maps carved into them.

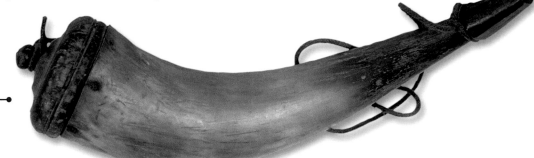

BULLET MOLDS

Between battles, soldiers often needed to make their own shot. They carried ball-shaped molds made of stone or iron for this job. They poured molten lead into the molds to make bullets.

SPYGLASSES

Some officers carried small telescopes called spyglasses. These devices helped them watch enemy movements from far away.

DRUMS

Armies of the 1700s usually marched with musicians. Drums were used to send signals to troops on the battlefield. A type of flute called a fife was used to inspire soldiers as they marched and fought.

COLORS

Each group of soldiers had its own flag, or colors. The color bearer was a soldier who carried the raised flag into battle. The flag showed a unit's position on the battlefield.

LONG-BARREL GUNS

Before the American Revolution, guns were heavy and hard to reload. Newer flintlock muskets were an improvement, but were still hard to load and shoot. The best guns were rifles. Twisting grooves called rifling were cut inside the barrel. Rifling made the shot spin as it was fired, which helped the bullet fly straighter and farther.

MUZZLE-LOADING MUSKETS

Muzzle-loading muskets were the most common weapon of the war. The shot was loaded in the open end, or muzzle, of the gun barrel. The typical musket was more than 4 feet (1.2 meters) long and weighed 8 to 12 pounds (3.6 to 5.4 kilograms).

FLINTLOCKS

Most guns at the time used a flintlock, which created a spark that fired the shot. Most soldiers could fire a flintlock musket three or four times a minute.

BATTLE FACT

The British musket was called the "Brown Bess" because of its brown, wooden stock. The name Bess might come from the German word *busche*, which means "bush".

CARBINES

Cavalry soldiers often used carbines. A carbine was shorter than a regular musket and fired slightly smaller shot. The carbine's lighter weight made it easier to carry and fire on horseback.

BREECH-LOADING RIFLES

British officer Patrick Ferguson perfected one of the world's first **breech**-loading rifles. Few were used during the war, perhaps because the British government did not realize how effective they were. Soldiers could fire faster when loading from the breech instead of the muzzle.

PENNSYLVANIA LONG RIFLES

Some American frontiersmen had guns called Pennsylvania long rifles. A good shooter could hit a target up to 200 yards (183 m) away with a Pennsylvania rifle. Common muskets were accurate only to about 50 yards (46 m). But the Pennsylvania was very slow to reload. For that reason, it was not very effective in battle.

 breech—the rear part of a gun behind the barrel

PISTOLS AND GRENADES

In addition to long-barreled guns, soldiers used several smaller weapons. Pistols fired accurately, but only at short distances. Grenades were small explosives that could be thrown or sometimes fired from special guns.

CAVALRY PISTOLS

Cavalry troops often kept two pistols strapped to their saddles. Officers carried them too, though the average foot soldier did not. The guns stayed in leather pouches called holsters until needed.

POCKET PISTOLS

Some officers carried smaller guns called pocket pistols. These were easily hidden in an officer's pocket. One American version of this gun was just 7.5 inches (19 centimeters) long.

PISTOLS AT SEA

Sailors usually hung their pistols on a hook on their belts. The guns were handy when boarding an enemy ship or for defending their own ship. The barrels of these handguns were made of brass, which resisted the damaging effect of seawater.

BLUNDERBUSS

Some sailors and marines used a blunderbuss. This short musket had a wide barrel end. The blunderbuss sprayed small shot over a wide area. It was an effective weapon against enemies on a crowded ship's deck.

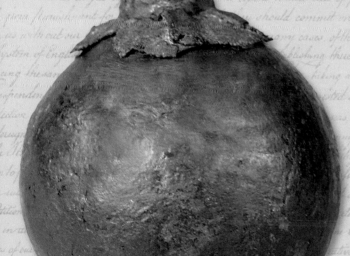

HAND GRENADES

A rarer small weapon was the hand grenade. A small, spherical iron container was filled with gunpowder. A soldier lit a fuse and then threw the grenade. When the lit fuse reached the powder, the grenade exploded.

SWORDS AND KNIVES

Thousands of years ago, people learned to create weapons from iron and steel. The metal allowed weapons to have both a cutting edge and a piercing point. During the American Revolution, both American and British soldiers used a variety of swords, knives, and other bladed weapons on the battlefield.

BAYONETS
A bayonet was one of a soldier's most important weapons. Most battles ended with enemies fighting in hand-to-hand combat. The bayonet turned a gun into a deadly spear with a long reach.

HUNTING SWORDS
Infantry troops carried straight swords. Some of these weapons were simple hunting swords used to kill an animal after it had been wounded.

CAVALRY SABERS
Cavalry soldiers favored swords called sabers. These slightly curved swords were ideal for soldiers on horseback when attacking enemy infantry troops.

LONG KNIVES

Soldiers also carried knives for a variety of uses. Riflemen often used long knives for hand-to-hand combat.

CUTLASSES

At sea, sailors used short swords called cutlasses. These smaller swords were ideal for close fighting on cramped ships.

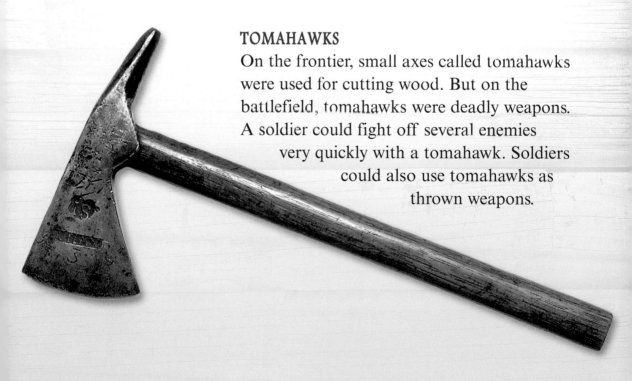

TOMAHAWKS

On the frontier, small axes called tomahawks were used for cutting wood. But on the battlefield, tomahawks were deadly weapons. A soldier could fight off several enemies very quickly with a tomahawk. Soldiers could also use tomahawks as thrown weapons.

ARTILLERY

Large guns came in different sizes and had different uses. Artillery guns were named according to the weight of the shot they fired. At the start of the war, Americans had few artillery pieces. Many of the large guns used by Americans were captured from the British during the war.

FIELD CANNON

The basic field cannon had a long metal barrel. It fired a cannonball on a fairly straight path over long distances. Sometimes the cannonball was fired so it would bounce along the ground to wipe out advancing enemy troops.

18-POUNDER SIEGE GUN

Heavier cannons, such as 18-pounders, were often used during sieges of enemy locations. The heavy guns usually stayed in one spot. Soldiers used them to fire large **shells** at targets.

 shell—a metal container filled with gunpowder and fired from a large gun; shells explode when they hit the ground

GRASSHOPPERS

The British had both 1.5- and 3-pound (0.6- and 1.4-kg) cannons that were sometimes called grasshoppers. The guns got this name because they tended to hop backward when fired.

SWIVEL GUN

The swivel gun was a small cannon. It was usually mounted on the side of a ship or the wall of a fort. Its barrel moved from side to side. Because of its small size, only two men were needed to load and fire it.

BATTLE FACT

Most artillery guns required up to five men to load, fire, and clean out the barrels between shots.

SPECIAL-USE ARTILLERY

Field guns were not useful in all situations. Some cannons could not be angled high enough to fire over an army's own troops. Military engineers came up with new designs that solved some of the limits of basic cannons.

MORTARS
Mortars had shorter and wider barrels than cannons. They were designed to fire shot or explosives at high angles over walls, trees, and friendly troops.

HOWITZERS
Howitzers had the best features of both cannons and mortars. They could fire at high angles like mortars. And they could fire at low angles like cannons. Howitzers could fire either solid shot or explosive shells.

NAVAL CANNONS

The carriages of naval cannons had small wheels. The guns only had to move short distances to be loaded and fired. The common 32-pounder weighed 5,500 pounds (2,495 kg).

CARRONADES

During the war the British developed a new naval cannon called a carronade. It was much lighter than most cannons, and it used less gunpowder. Nicknamed the "Smasher," a carronade could fire 68-pound (31-kg) shot.

COEHORNS

Some ships also carried coehorns. These small mortars were designed to be easily carried and fired.

FIRING THE BIG GUNS

Soldiers had to stand clear as they fired large artillery guns. The force of the shot could send the heavy gun and its carriage rolling back several feet. Unlike most ground troops, artillery gunners could fire several kinds of projectiles, depending on the targets.

CANNONBALL

Solid iron cannonballs could blast through the sides of wooden ships or buildings. Just one of these heavy balls could take out several enemy soldiers.

GRAPESHOT AND CANISTER

Canisters held many small iron balls called grapeshot. The balls spread out over a wide area after they were fired. They could hit several enemy troops at once.

projectile—an object that is thrown or shot through the air

EXPLOSIVE SHELL

Explosives were also used as projectiles. Gunners lit the fuse of an iron ball filled with gunpowder. The shell exploded over enemy troops. Those who weren't killed were showered with bits of hot metal.

CARCASS

A carcass was a shot covered or filled with **flammable** material that was lit before it was fired. Carcasses were usually used to set wooden buildings on fire.

CHAIN SHOT

Chain shot was sometimes used on ships. It cut through an enemy ship's ropes and sails.

flammable—likely to catch fire

WARFARE ON THE WATER

At the start of the war, the British and American navies were very different. The Americans had merchant ships but no real warships. The British had battleships with as many as 70 guns and 500 sailors. Captains often didn't like sinking enemy ships unless it was necessary. They simply wanted to capture the other vessel and anything useful it had on board.

SHIPS OF THE LINE
These were the largest fighting ships of the day. They could have up to three decks and as many as 120 guns. The heavier guns were placed on the lowest deck, with lighter guns on the upper decks.

UNDERWATER OBSTACLES
Americans used dangerous underwater obstacles to try to block British ships from sailing up rivers. One such obstacle was the spiked timber crib. Wooden timbers created a small pen that held large rocks. The rocks held up a large spike that could pierce the bottom of an enemy ship.

FLOATING BATTERIES

The floating battery was not really a ship. It looked more like a small fort that floated on a raft and held guns. Sailors would usually row them into place, but a few also used sails.

UNDERWATER MINES

Underwater mines were deadly explosive devices. A mine could blast a hole in a ship's hull, sinking it and removing it from battle.

BATTLE FACT

American David Bushnell built the *Turtle*, the first submarine. It was made to attach mines to the underside of British ships. The *Turtle* failed in its mission. But successful submarines were later based on the *Turtle's* design.

GLOSSARY

breech (BREECH)—the rear part of a gun behind the gun's barrel

cavalry (KA-vuhl-ree)—a group of soldiers who travel and fight on horseback

colonist (KAH-luh-nist)—a person who settles in a new territory that is governed by his or her home country, the settled area is called a colony

flammable (FLA-muh-buhl)—likely to catch fire

frontier (fruhn-TIHR)—the far edge of a settled area, where few people live

infantry (IN-fuhn-tree)—a group of soldiers trained to fight and travel on foot

militia (muh-LISH-uh)—a group of volunteer citizens organized to fight, but who are not professional soldiers

projectile (pruh-JEK-tuhl)—an object, such as a bullet or missile, that is thrown or shot through the air

shell (SHEL)—a metal container filled with gunpowder and fired from a large gun; shells exploded when they hit the ground

READ MORE

Micklos, John Jr. *From Thirteen Colonies to One Nation.* Revolutionary War Library. Berkeley Heights, N.J.: Enslow Elementary, 2008.

Murray, Stuart. *American Revolution.* DK Eyewitness Books. New York: DK Pub., in association with the Smithsonian Institution, 2005.

Raum, Elizabeth. *The Revolutionary War: An Interactive History Adventure.* You Choose. Mankato, Minn.: Capstone Press, 2010.

INTERNET SITES

FactHound offers a safe, fun way to find Internet sites related to this book. All of the sites on FactHound have been researched by our staff.

Here's all you do:

Visit *www.facthound.com*

Type in this code: 9781429676472

INDEX